New Island / New Drama   *Series Editor* / Dermot Bolger

CATALPA

CATALPA
Donal O'Kelly

New Island Books / Dublin
Nick Hern Books / London

Catalpa

is first published in 1997 by

New Island Books

2, Brookside,

Dundrum Road,

Dublin 14,

Ireland

and in Britain by

Nick Hern Books

14 Larden Road

London W3 7ST

ISBN 1 874597 57X (NIB)

1 85459 3579 (NHB)

New Island Books receives financial assistance from
The Arts Council (An Chomhairle Ealaíon)
Dublin, Ireland.

Cover illustration by Jon Berkeley
Cover photo of Donal O'Kelly
by Marc Marnie / Stagefright
Typeset by Graphic Resources
Printed in Ireland by Colour Books Ltd.

BIOGRAPHICAL NOTE

Born in Dublin in 1958, Donal O'Kelly is a playwright and actor. His plays include *Asylum! Asylum!*, *The Dogs*, and his widely-travelled one-man play *Bat The Father Rabbit The Son*. As an actor, he is best known for his starring role as Bimbo in Roddy Doyle's *The Van*. In 1995, he performed Beckett's *Act Without Words I* in the Gate Theatre's Beckett Festival at the Lincoln Centre, New York.

INTRODUCTION

Catalpa has been through quite a voyage since it first set sail.

In 1992, Dublin's Rough Magic Theatre Company sent me to Australia with my one-man play *Bat The Father Rabbit The Son*. While playing the Perth Festival, I heard a little about Fremantle but never got around to visiting the jail, which apparently is now a museum.

But when I came back to Dublin, I was browsing one day in the Winding Stair bookshop when I came across Sean Ó Luing's excellent account of the Catalpa rescue, *Fremantle Mission*. What a wonderful story, I thought.

I went digging, and discovered that George Anthony, who captained the Catalpa voyage, actually published his own story in 1897, *The Catalpa Expedition*, written by a journalist acquaintance called Zephaniah Pease. The National Library kindly photocopied the book for me, one of only three hundred printed. Then there was John Devoy's serialisation of the rescue mission in his newspaper, *The Gaelic American,* in 1904. This was mostly based on legendary Fenian John Breslin's version of events, and had an understandable eye towards the propaganda value of recalling the daring Catalpa story almost thirty years later, at a time of rising support for Irish nationalism.

Then came the letter from Australia. It was a newspaper cutting about recently-discovered letters and poems of John Boyle O'Reilly, but in the bottom corner was a reference to a book, *The Fenians in Australia 1865-1880* by Keith Amos. I asked around, and hunted down what was apparently one of only a few copies in Ireland in the Gilbert Library in Pearse Street. Here was the stuff of human drama. Amos had access to the police files of the time, the hundred-year embargo having elapsed. Not that I'd believe everything I'd read in a police file, but the story of Breslin and Marie Tondut, the French girl he fell in love with, is so bizarre that it must be largely true.

The motor on which *Catalpa* drives is a question: What is a hero? This question has been at the heart of Western culture since the time of the Greeks. Mostly it's avoided. Cliched storylines that avoid ambiguity and shun complexity are the norm. The end result is a proliferation of *Rambo*-like storylines which infect human development in a very debilitating way. Now I had a story which could challenge the hero myth using all the tried and tested storytelling elements of the ancient hero's journey.

The next stage was deciding how to tell the story. The obvious way was to write a movie. But a storyline like *Catalpa* would be a multi-million dollar blockbuster, with all the conservative ramifications that entails. It looked a nightmare scenario to me. No realistic possibility of delving into the wonderful complexity of being human and being heroic along that path, I thought. Then a tantalising idea started to grow. Why not do it myself? After all, *Bat The Father Rabbit The Son* was a play about two people in the same body, the son being inhabited from time to time by the father. The theatrical challenge had been to convince the audience to believe that two people were before them, and it largely worked. Ever since, I'd wanted to take it a step further, present a full cast of characters — progress logically from schizophrenia to polyphrenia — and here I had an epic storyline to accommodate that. What if this story and all these characters were to inhabit the mind of a screenwriter ... and I get to play the whole damn lot!?

On the 2nd of May 1995, the first production of *Catalpa — The Movie*, by Red Kettle Theatre Company in Waterford parted from the dock and set sail.

Donal O'Kelly

Note: Many people have contributed to the writing and rewriting of *Catalpa*. Director Bairbre Ní Chaoimh obviously had an enormous input. Tich Meagher and Trevor Knight also contributed. Jim Nolan, Red Kettle's artistic director, was extremely helpful at the nerve-wracked pre-opening stage first time around. And Michael Colgan and Anne Clarke of the Gate were of great assistance in rewriting for the new production — the version published here. Sincere thanks to them all, because theatre is rooted in the collaborative pursuit of excellence, and to all the others who were involved in the process along the way.

Catalpa — The Movie was first produced by Red Kettle Theatre Company in the Garter Lane Theatre, Waterford, in May 1995.

Performed by	Donal O'Kelly
Directed by	Bairbre Ní Chaoimh
Designed by	Ben Hennessy
Music Composed and Performed by	Trevor Knight

The Gate Theatre Dublin production of *Catalpa* — the version published here — was first produced in March 1997. Donal O'Kelly, Bairbre Ní Caoimh and Trevor Knight performed, directed and composed the music. Giles Cadle designed the Gate production.

STAGING CATALPA

The real Catalpa expedition was a glittering triumph in the midst of the colossal failure of the Fenian movement. The triumph of failure is a cliché of Irish history. So it was more than fitting to couch this *Catalpa* story in the setting of failure — the failure of a would-be screenwriter to pitch his story satisfactorily. I could have almost subtitled the play "What I should have said was ..."

Matthew Kidd's bedsitter is the setting. The theatrical challenge is to flick images into the audience's heads, to stimulate their imaginations so that they will see the Catalpa at sea, they will see and hear and feel and smell the Atlantic swell, the whale blubber, the scorched Australian shore. The instruments used to do this are the text itself — the images described, the bits of dialogue, the words used, the sounds, with movement, gesture, energy, stillness, with music sometimes, with lighting, and the use of a few select props. But the main function of all of these is to kick-start the most important instrument of all: the audience's imagination.

The only furniture in Matthew Kidd's bedsit are a table, a chair, a bed, and a trunk. These are all used to represent different places and things from time to time: the bed becomes the Catalpa, the chair a horse-and-trap and so on. A few domestic objects are also used: a bowl, a pair of boots, salt and pepper shakers, a towel, a box of matches, a chain, a silk bedspread, a gauze curtain.

To include stage directions in this text would only serve to confuse. We developed our way of using a few objects to trigger the audience's imagination, to communicate the written text as fully as possible. Another set of people could choose totally different props, used in a totally different way, which might well be just as effective.

In the text, in order to make it clear that the entire story takes place in Matthew Kidd's imagination, and is delivered by a solo performer, the characters' names appear in a smaller point size.

ACT ONE

Nightime. A shabby bedsit. A bed, a table, a chair. A long muslin curtain hanging from the outline of a large window. Matthew Kidd in pyjamas.

Matthew: Sick of it! I'm sick of it!
I'm sick of it! Sick to death of it!
Sick of it I'm sick to death of it!
Stuck in a rut that never ends!
Rooting around on the shitpile!
Sludge sludge slithery drudgery -
There's got to be more to -
Life's Great Mystery
Than a trail of missed chances I didn't even see
And Muffed Opportunities!
All a terrible mistake
From day fucking one
To now -
Wipe it out and start again!
If only I fucking well could.
Try try and try again ...
Prayer of the perpetual failure!
Try try and - Jesus Christ!
How did I develop such capacity for fuck-up?
Hereditary? No!
All the family have a good firm grip
on what my father called
The Forces Of Life!
They all have proper jobs and comfortable homes.
Then I come along all arrogance and boldly striking out -
pioneering new horizons,
taking the art of the cinema to previously unscaled heights:-
Matthew Kidd, Oscar-winning screenwriter of -
Catalpa! The Greatest Movie ... ...
never made!

To this final indignity,
the last crucifying straw,
because I sat there,
mute,
on my arse,
facing those tinseltown know-it-all morons from
Hollywood -
Just trust me I wanted to say.
Buy my screenplay,
give me the cash,
and shoot the movie to make all of our
Dreams Come True!
But instead - turned hostile.
Could feel my face tighten, my eyes go cold.
Tried to talk - civil, but that old outstanding vein
in my temple betrayed me -
Always does! Judas vein! Throbbing in anger!
Try to - relax and seem at ease
but they know I hate them.
Try to look nonchalant ... I meet Hollywood
producers every day of the week - yawn ...
Foolish man!
Foolish foolish man!
What I could have said was ...
What I should have said was ...
Why didn't I just **show** them ...
The pictures in my head ...
Why didn't I -

Matthew changes into a gwawking seabird. The lighting changes to suggest the change from the sad grey world of Matthew's bedsit to the vibrant technicolour world of his imagination.

Gwawk-kwawk! Gwawk-kwawk!
Seabird. Gwawk.
I'm a long wet seabird. Kwawk.
I am a seabird, long-necked and wet,
and I'm squatting on your desk

Mister Big Picture Movieman.
My feathers drip.
Puddles form between my feet,
but I'm still proud.
I puff out my breast and I impress you.
And now, I'm going to fly.
I'm going to spread my wings and fly in the sky.
Come with me Movieman from Hollywood.
Anyone can fly.
Just spread your wings and flap
then dive and haul ...
fwip fwip fwip fwip fwip fwip
Waves.
Choppy choppy waves green-brown tossing
toss-schloss waves.
Breast feathers flutter in the harsh sea wind.
Fwip.
Cliffs loom ahead.
Say a fish still wriggles in your - in your bill!
Fwip.
Bank up and sweep starboard towards -
Screen caption:
New Bedford, Massachussetts, April 1875.
Hold caption as the slate grey sky darkens,
lamps start to dimly glow,
windows start to twinkle - fwip,
over the port you glide,
the masts of the stocky whaling-vessels draw
strange loops as the ships pitch and bob,
sailors roll the barrels of oil down onto the dock,
you wing your way above the town,
over the rollicking bars,
and over the desperate shacks,
wow-whoooow a lean mongrel bays,
a boy throws a stick at you but misses by a mile
because - you're too high ...
fwip
you climb towards the plush slopes of the
whaling-agents' mansions overlooking the town
fwip
the fish wriggles again ...

There's Gretta down below,
beautiful Gretta,
with sadness in her so-sweet smile -
think of - Winona could do it and Julia'd be fine
but best of all would be Michelle, yes, Michelle.
Beautiful Gretta but steely too as we shall see
plays with pretty little baby daughter Pearl
on the manicured lawns of her father's house.
She's dressed in - flowing crimson,
but she's not stuffy
no she's free-spirited
she doesn't mind kneeling on the damp dark
grass arms extended like - angel's wings:-
- run, she shouts sweetly,
she doesn't care that Pearl can only crawl she's
looking ahead to the happy future when Pearl
will -
twirl and - pirouette with the joy she'll feel of
that Gretta is perfectly certain my little
love-Pearl ...
Fwip!
Suddenly the fish.
Lashes.
Flips.
Falls.
Flops onto the lawn between Gretta and - !
Hands to face!
A fish on grass - how strange!
Looks up darkly.
Picks up Pearl.
A thing of the sea has come to me ...

Gwawk!
Fwip fwip fwip fly higher seabird,
fly away from there,
whe-e-e-el
to hover over the drab sagging rusty structure of -
the Morse Twist Drill Works.
Zoom in close to an upstairs window in the
primitive office of clerks,

where a young man observes you through a
telescope - Kevin Costner or Tom Cruise -
you flap your wings and rise
but George Anthony - for it is he -
keeps the telescope trained on the dark grey
horizon.
A whaling-ship enters the bay,
hull low with kill.
- The sea, the sea Gretta, the sea ...
The Morse Twist Drill Works,
the Morse Twist Drill works,
Nuts bolts screws drills latches hinges grommets
locks,
Nuts bolts screws drills latches hinges grommets
locks,
George pens the entries in - the Morse Twist
Drill Works,
scratch scratch scratch scratch down the page
the columns inch,
Scratch, scratch, scratch - Ah!

But last night,
standing on the landing of their modest little
house,
looking out to sea,
poor Pearl teething - the molars at the back -
round red cheeks ...

George: Ssh, stop it Pearl, that's enough you'll wake the
dead. Look at the moon on the peaceful sea ...

Gretta fussing all bustle in the flounces of her
nightdress -

Gretta: Give her to me you're useless with her -

George: Useless!? I was the one who woke.

Gretta: Useless! She's not a sailor you can spit your
orders at!

George: Uh-oh you're tired, Gretta, tired -

Gretta:	Tired of you with the blasted sea in your dreamy eyes while your daughter cries her heart out for your attention -
George:	I'm trying to make her stop -
Gretta:	And the house falls down around our ears -
George:	I'm doing the best I can.
Gretta:	Stop running away from her! Stop sailing secretly out of that bay!
George:	Stop your stupid talk woman!
Gretta:	Don't call me woman! Call me Gretta! Call me love!
George:	Ssh Pearl Momma doesn't mean to shout.
Gretta:	Go away to sea again! Damn you First Mate Anthony the Great! Release the three of us from this!
George:	You know why I can't do that! Why taunt me Gretta!? You want me to spit on your mother's grave!?
George:	Can you live if you don't George ... !?

(Pause)

George:	Little Pearl's nodded off now.
Gretta:	Put her gently into her cot ... and come into the sea with me George ... ...
George:	Gretta ...
Gretta:	Ssh ...

Put her gently into her cot soft and easy, sleep, Pearl, sleep ...

Gretta:	Come into the soft sea bed George ... the sea, the sea, George, the sea ... duckdown featherbed ... ...

Duckdown featherbed!
Strange that Gretta's mother chose
such a wedding-gift to give!
A year since she held my hand as she coughed
and spat to force the words from her cracked
blue lips:-

Momma: Promise me,
I'm on my deathbed,
promise me you'll never go to sea!
Promise me you'll stay by Gretta's side!
She loves you too much -
she loves you, you hear!?
She loves you dangerously, dangerous you hear!?
You mustn't go away if you break her heart I'll
haunt you ...
you mustn't go away I'll come back from death
like a spirit like a ghost and I'll seek you out and
find you however far you go George Anthony!
I'll haunt you
and destroy you
 if you
sail out to
sea again
if you
break
my
daughter
Gretta's
heart!

The sea, the sea, Gretta, the sea Gretta, the sea.
Cut to:

The Morse Twist Drill Works
George slams ledger shut
pan to window
external
pony-trap
top-hatted pair of gentlemen approach
clippa-cloppa clippa-cloppa
Closeup:

Wooden spokes wet gravel crunch splash.
Trap's wooden spokes stop.
Gretta's father, New Bedford's biggest
whaling-agent John T. Richardson alights. Patent
leather shoe plunges into rust-ringed puddle.

Richardson: Shit! Shoe's wet.

Henry Hathaway port commissioner always
ready to laugh pats his hat and sniggers.

Hathaway: Put your foot in it, did you Jonty-hee-hee!?

Door tinkle-ding bang!

Morse: Mister Richardson! Mister Hathaway!

Richardson: Evening Morse!

Morse: To what do I owe the -

Richardson: My son-in-law. Tell him it's urgent!

Morse: Why certainly Mr. Richardson -

Skip skip skip two-at-a-time

Morse: Geo-orge!

Shuffle shuffle footsteps above and -

Richardson: Come with us George! We'd like to talk to you.

George: Gretta will be expecting me for tea.

Richardson: Get in the trap George. We need to talk.

Get-in-the-trap get-in-the-trap get-in-the- ... !!
Pony-trappa clippa-cloppa clippa-cloppa
down in the dusk to the docks.
Barques in the bay dark as pitch -
look at the whaler George had watched just
docked,
barrels rolling offa timberolla waff-waff
waves washing the dock splosh!
Clippa-cloppa clippa-cloppa

down dark sidestreets
trap scrapes the wooden walls ...

George: I'll call on Gretta, let her know ...

Richardson: No time to stop George!

Clippa-cloppa clippa-cloppa
Gwawk-kwawk! Fwip fwip fwip fwip ...

Richardson: For ten year you were the best seaman in my
employ George. That's unqualified.

- Unqualified, says Hathaway.

Clippa-clop -

Richardson: The long and the short of it is:- I want you back
at sea George.

- Back where you belong ah-ha, says Hathaway.

George: I can't go back to sea sir.

Richardson: I'm offering you a captaincy. Your own
whaling-ship George. Captain's percentage on
every kill. What do you say?

Nyaahahaha!

Jarvey: Easy gurl easy! Sorry sirs the horse is frighted!

Clippa-cloppa clippa-cloppa

George: Why are you offering me a captaincy?

Richardson: To save you from a life of nuts and bolts!

- Nuts and bolts, man dear, says Hathaway, a life
of nuts and bolts ...

What does he want clippa-cloppa
after trying to stop my marriage to his daughter
clippa-cloppa
now he offers me a captaincy ... !?

Clippock-clock whoa!

Richardson: She's beautiful, isn't she?

Backwater dock.

Richardson: Take the lamp and look George!

Lift the lamp to reveal faded name on yellow
hull just behind the jib-boom - Catalpa.

Richardson: Want to board?

Nyaahahaha ...
fwip fwip fwip fwip ...
you prom - issed me ...
Gangway thunk thunk thunk
eergh-ck-ck ... eergh-ck-ck ...

- She's beautiful, thinks George, she's a dream
vessel ...

Richardson: Go into the cabin George ...

Hathaway: That's right, the cabin George ah-ha ...

Eergh ...
Dark. Lighted taper. Lamp flares.

George: Who the Hell is this!?

Richardson: George I'd like you to meet Mister John Devoy
of Ireland. He has some business to discuss.

Introductions. Strained pleasantries.
Richardson and Hathaway smoke on deck.

Broad black brimmer, hollow cheeks, long black
bushy beard, black cape, black eyes piercing in
the dark, thin white hand extended to shake -
crunch!

Devoy: Devoy devoy devoy apoc-a-lippa poc-a-lippa
poc-a-lasha lippa-laddy-oh ...

apoc-a-lippa poc-a-lippa poc-a-lasha
lippa-laddy-oh ... !
Devoy devoy de - Manacles!
Ten years ago shimmer shimmer ...
in the land of my birth shimmer shimmer ...
revolution freedom throw the yoke of oppresh -

shimmer shimmer into flashback.
Fighting Fenians wait for the word to rise up and
strike the blow that'll break the grip of the
Saxon knave.
Even Irishmen in the British Army swear their
allegiance to the secret Fenian army the IRB -
Irish Republican Brotherhood brotherhood
brotherhood sinister music to suit.
High wideshot cramped attic of Dublin pub,
hunched backs in whispered sedition,
zoom down and in on central bunch of six in
British Army uniforms bibles in hand:-
- I swear, in the name of God,
Cranston, Darragh, Hassett, Hogan, Harrington
and Wilson,
- and in the name of the dead generations ...
Door bursts in,
soldiers and polis they swarm,
chaotic with panic and fear:
- Erin go bree-raw ree-raw ...
skittenda slappetta pitcheta rickety-racketin
ladder-an-steps ducketa-pucketa trap-door
slither in under the roofbeams ...
to be clamped!
Fade into sunlit courtroom
- Deportation to the Penal Colony of Western
Australia, there to Endure Penal Servitude for
Life.
Fade into awful voyage
deep in the hold of the transportation ship
Cranston Darragh Hassett Hogan Harrington and
Wilson,
in legchains and manacles,
nya-kithendy-nyaah kithendy-nyaaah ...

Whoa-woh-woh
didgeridoo-de-didgeridoo-woowoh-woo ...
Whoa-woh-woh
didgeridoo-de-didgeridoo-woowoh-woo ...
Fade into scorched Australian bush.
Six pairs of leaden legs in busted boots
crunch crunch crunch -
Cabin of Catalpa:
Black piercing eyes:

Devoy: Ten years is enough, Mister Anthony.

George: Undoubtedly.

Devoy: They must be rescued, Mister Anthony.

George: Undoubtedly.

Devoy: You must captain the Catalpa on a rescue voyage!

George: You make assumptions sir!

Devoy: Richardson!

Out on the after-deck, facing out to sea:

Richardson: We all gain, George.

George: I can't go back to sea sir!

Richardson: I know Gretta's got a - thing about the sea ...

George: I promised Gretta's mother on her deathbed sir. You know that.

Richardson: She was always a flexible woman George. I'll always give her that. ... Listen to me! This is your chance in life. Seize it or you'll live a lifetime of ledger-filling to regret it. Half the purse George! Captain the Catalpa and half the profits from the whale-hunting on the voyage are yours. You're the best whaler New Bedford's ever had! You'll make your fortune George - in just one voyage. Just one, George. ... Then you'll be in a position to take care of my

daughter Gretta in the way that she's
accustomed to.

George: I've never asked you for anything! Neither has
she!

Richardson: Her crimson dress is patched at the helm! My
daughter is wearing a patch, George!

George: What's in it for you!?

Richardson: I'm in commerce George. Whales won't last
forever. But Irish-America will. I need to spread
my bets. The future's in it for me.

George: Supposing I accept ...

Richardson: You'll be sworn to silence. Absolutely
unconditional.

George: What about Gretta?

Richardson: We'll take good care of Gretta. I promise you.

- That we will, says ear-wigging Hathaway,
we'll take good care of Gretta, rest assured
ah-ha-ha-ha-ha-ha ...

Clippa-cloppa clippa-cloppa ponytrappa stoppa
droppa George

Richardson: G'night.

George: 'Night ... clippa cloppa clippa cloppa ...

George enters dark, tiptoes up the stairs, stands
on the creaky landing, looking out the window
at the sea.
The sea. Sigh. Closeup.

George: Those six men. Such injustice. Very sad.
Half the profits, he said.
money isn't everything of course.
The Morse Twist Drill Works, dry land position,
supplies enough. Just.
But that leak has to be fixed.

One voyage he said.
That patch! Gretta poor Gretta!
She has a weakness for the best satins and silks.
Feminine. Nice. Mmm Gretta's satins and silks.
She deserves them.
She deserves to have them.
She deserves more!

From the pillow sleepy voice ...

Gretta: Where were you George? Pearl missed you. I
missed you. Where were you *petit Georges* ... ?

Sometimes, she used the French.
Rustle rustle.
Satins and silks she loves, she loves,
against her skin she says.
rustle rustle-shiff

Gretta: Come into the dark sea *Georges* ... *Geo-orges* ...

Sailing,
skimming on the surface of that gentle
feather-bed,
the heaving swell of the duckdown, duck
down ...
swish rustle-and-shiff,
ebb-tide, full-tide, tilt to the port side,
heave-to and tumble-lunge,
sounding, sounding,
salty undersea caves,
humpback and sperm whale, coming up for air,
rorqual and narwhal,
Sei whales and Minke whales,
Blue whales and Right whales -
Jonah's Dining Hall ...

George: Gretta, oh Gretta ...

Gretta: Don't talk -

George: Gretta -

Gretta: Silence in the deep *Georges! Ne parle pas!*

George: Gretta the sea -

Gretta: Yes my love, come into the sea my manwhale -

George: Gretta, the sea, I'm going away to sea!

Yah! Grrr-ett-ah! Fucketa pucketa outa de bed.
Cut to:
Bottom of stairs.
George, naked, hands guarding bobbing member.
One boot hurtles down, stud -ouch! splits his
eyebrow.

George: Stop it, Gretta, stop, you'll wake the -

Gretta: You care about our baby!? You're deserting her!

George: No! I'm doing this for her. And for you Gretta!

Gretta: What are you doing that excuses leaving me
alone!?

George: I can't tell you Gretta but it won't be for long.

Gretta: You can't tell me!? I'm your wife!

George: It's a secret Gretta.

Gretta: You've made your choice George!

Naked, at the top of the stairs, points down,
gloriously crazed, magnificent, tempestuous.

Gretta: You've chosen the sea. Unfaithful man! I
thought you were different, but no! Go and
embrace her! But be warned! She's a tease. And
be careful what you catch! She's had a million
foolhardy men ram their way through her before
she captured you!

Wraps herself in crimson silk.

Gretta: You'll never sail these seas again. *Adieu!*
Georges!

Tosses second boot. It clunks into the
grandfather clock - the only wedding gift from

Richardson to which they would agree. We're
independent, they'd said, come what may.
George looks at himself in the glass pendulum
case.
Marked.
Tic toc tic toc tic toc ... you'll never sail ... these
seas ... again ...

Fadeup background noise.
Public house backroom Devoy all smiles arm
around George's shoulder -

Devoy: Voy devoy devoyde
howde proud I am **Captain!** Anthony to
introduce you to John Breslin here, just arrived
from dirty Dublin city and a braver man devoy
devoy devoyde -

Big thickset fellow with a grandee walrus
moustache and his head set in such a way as to
insist he's an upright and honourable gent who
brooks no knaves but who'll give every man his
chance to prove he's made of the finer elements
of that mysterious concoction to which we tend
to refer as the human character. Keeps referring
lasciviously to the proprietor's buxom wife, and
even when not so referring, tracks her with his
eyes shaded between his bushy eyebrows and
his sprouting moustache.
Devoy lowers his voice and they all lean in.

Devoy: This is the plan, men. George here picks his
crew and sets sail as if on a normal North
Atlantic whaling voyage. Then he bears south,
across the Equator, round the African Cape,
across the Indian Ocean, to the shores of
Western Australia. Meanwhile, Breslin here will
take the other route. Steamtrain to San Francisco
John - avoid Chief Sitting Bull at all costs we
wouldn't want you scalped - then, steamship
from San Francisco across the Pacific to Sydney,
travel across to Western Australia, make contact

with the prisoners, and ready them for rescue as soon as the Catalpa arrives. The rest I'll leave to you two gentlemen to plan. John:

Breslin: Right! As and from this point in time, my name is not John Breslin. My name, *(changes to deep southern accent)* is Mister James Collins, and I'm pleased to introduce myself to you gentlemen as a business speculator in mining interests. I don't mind telling both of you I intend to extract some valuable stock from the shores of Western Australia. *(Back to normal accent)* Ah-ha ha laugh laugh grin cough grimace swallow phlegm and stroke moustache.

George: One thing must be clear.

Devoy: Eh what's that George?

George: What Mister Bres- ... what Mister **Collins** does on the shore in Australia is up to him - I have full confidence he'll fulfil his purpose. But while we're at sea, I command the Catalpa, and therefore I command this mission.

Devoy: Devoy devoy devoyde hmm ... well, I don't see why that should create insurmountable difficulties for anyone. Do you, Breslin- Collins- Mister- what the blazes - James ... !?

Breslin: I can't think, of a circumstance, here and now, off the top of my head, where it could ...

George: That's agreed then ... ?

Devoy: You have our word of honour George. I give you my commitment. Fadevoy defadedevoy defadevoy defade ...

George: I'm going away Pearl,
I know you don't understand Poppa,
but I have to go away to sea and leave you for a while.
Poppa loves you Pearl,
and he loves your momma too,
but he's been given a difficult choice,

and he's chosen a way to put things right,
instead of struggling along
with things going wrong -
creaking boards, leaking roof, Gretta's patched
hem ... !
Poppa'll be back to hold you tight,
and Poppa and Momma'll be happy together
with you Pearl,
and you'll sing for us - a sea song,
and Gretta will smile
and we'll all be fine, Pearl ...

Pull back to reveal Gretta, watching, listening,
moves slowly towards him, crimson silk flowing,
heart - beat, heart - beat,
staring into each other's eyes ...

Gretta: How's your - eyebrow, George?

George: It's fine Gretta, just a scratch ...

Si - lence deep!
Thum-thum! Rap on the door. Devoy's voice
- George!
They stare two three four ...
Thum-thum!
- George! Open up!
Pearl cries. Gretta stares.

George: You'll have to hold her while I answer that
            Gretta!
            - You've answered it already, she said!

Devoyde voyde voyde headless chicken voy
devoy devoy de

Devoy: Damn committeemen George! Over a barrel I
            am! The voyage is off!

George: The voyage is off!? What do you mean!?

Devoy: The whole plan is off, unless - ... ah!

George: Unless what!?

Devoy: Unless you take a Fenian in the crew.

George: The crew is already picked!

Devoy: I know! Damn tragic! Those six men - in
            manacles! - to have their hopes raised only to be
            dashed! Can you do anything to save them
            George!?

George: It means firing a hired man! It means creating
            discontent before we even start!

Devoy: I have a man. Duggan. He's a coach-builder.

George: A coach-builder!? On a whaling-ship!?

Devoy: Ship's carpenter, I thought. Stretching a point I
            know ...

            tic toc tic toc

Devoy: if not, the voyage is off!

            tic toc tic -

George: Alright! Duggan's the ship's carpenter.
            Satisfied!?

Devoy: Thank you George. From the bottom of my
            heart! Damn committees George! You've no
            idea! Cut - throat!! Devoyde voyde voyde voyde
            'night

George: 'Night.

Devoy: George! Manacles! Lest you forget wherefore
            you go. Goodnight.

            Tic toc tic toc tic toc
            you've answered it already she said,
            you'll never sail, these seas again,
            whaley-whale, whaley -

            Stow the anchor-chains!
            Thunk-thunka rolla-rolla tchink-tchink
            thunka-thunka rolla-rolla tchink-tchink
            busy-busy

Mop-sy! Tobey! Malay! Pawnee! Lopez!
First Mate Smith standing on the poopdeck:
- Foretopsail!!
Pulla rigga-ropey rigga-ropey rigga-ropey
rigga-ropey-oh!
Pulla rigga-ropey rigga-ropey rigga-ropey
rigga-ropey-oh!
- Maintopsail!!
Maintopsail flutter and flappeta furl-lurl-lurla
flah-whap!

Smith: You've chosen well, Captain Anthony. They're a first-rate crew.

George: Your job as First Mate is to ensure they're first-rate at sea, Mister Smith.

Smith: They're the best! They know your reputation. They're in it for their fraction of what they judge will be one mighty catch.

George: Let's hope their judgement's vindicated.

On the dockside:
Ponytrappa clippeta clippeta clop clop whoa!

Richardson: God speed, George. Safe voyage my boy!

- Six of the best of beasts at least, says
Hathaway
a-ha-ha-ha-ha-ha-ha ...

George stays impassive standing on the capstan.
Thunk-thunka Duggan hammer chisel
working on the whaleboat gunwhales
winks to Devoy standing at the pawnshop corner
doffs black brimmer in reply.
Pulla rigga-ropey rigga-ropey rigga-ropey
rigga-ropey-oh
Catalpa parts from the dock-splosh
stem to sea she plies
Nyaahahahaha the pony's taken fright
clattering onto the cobbles and muck
eyes gone wild

Cat - alpa Cat - alpa Cat - alpa
Fwip fwip fwip fwip
Suddenly a cry:
George looks back.
Gretta, on the quayside,
crimson dress that has the patch,
with Pearl, wailing, screeching like a seabird,
Gretta just stares,
- so you know wherefore you go George ...

George: Spanker and jibsail, Mister Smith!

Smith: Spanker and jibsail!!

Pulla rigga-ropey rigga-ropey rigga-ropey
rigga-ropey-oh
Pulla rigga-ropey rigga-ropey rigga-ropey
rigga-ropey-oh
The choppy sea the choppy sea the choppy sea
the sound of the sea ...
George ...
you pro - missed me ...
you'd never go to sea ...
she loves you dan-gerously ...
dan-gerous you see ...
you pro - missed me ...
you'd never go to sea ...
on my deathbed! On my deathbed!
Geo-orge Anthony ... Geo-orge Anthony ...
Geo-orge Anthony ....

Atlan-tic O-cean ... Atlan-tic O-cean ...
day into night into day into night
calm
the stars above
the sea beneath
the Catalpa tacking between
calm
the crew crouch together in the shelter of
the poopdeck the poopdeck the poopdeck ca-cha
whalers' songs they sing-a-ling-a
squeeze-e-box e squeeze-e-box

whaley-whale whaley-whale
Mopsy Tobey Malay Pawnee Lopez
Brava Gingy Lombard and Kanaka
First Mate Smith and
Second Mate Da Silva with his
squeeze-e-box e squeeze-e-box
whaley-whale squeeze-e-box
whaley-whale squeeze-e-box
Pull back and rise to show
faintly lit Catalpa
carving through the dark horses
of the night Atlan-tic the night Atlan-tic ...
Whaley-whale ... whaley-whale
Close in on single figure standing on the stern.
George stares at the starlit sea.
Lest I forget, he thinks, wherefore I go ...
So you know wherefore you go!
Gretta on the quayside!
Shouldn't have looked back!
Hathaway there to comfort here!
We'll take care of her well, a-ha ...
Back in New Bedford! New Bedford!
Whaley-whaley ... whaley-whale
Crew humming to their quarters dog-tired
spy the captainman staring from the stern!
Ssh.
Mopsy say:
- He make the magic. He trail the whale.
Brava say:
- He shake the sack with the chinky chain.
But Pawnee say:
- No! He dream! Make trouble to dream at sea!
- Ssh, Mopsy whisper, shh, let him listen to the
whale-hum ... ssh ...

First time he saw her,
heart of winter on the quayside,
warm in her bonnet and muff
with her mother in the trap
skidding through the slush
in a fresh snowfall.

He on the blubber-deck,
just a skinny boy,
boiling the last of the catch,
while the rest of the crew
spent their - relief
in the tavern where his mother used to work!
It's just a scratch Gretta. Just a scratch.
Snowflakes fell.
He saw her face beneath the bonnet lace.
Thought it was the least he could do to remove
his hat ...
She smiled.
Slush.
Blubber.
Blood.
She smiled.
Mother's arm turns her firmly away
and the trap jerks into motion
up the hill to home.
Mother's arm,
warmly protective,
warding off the seamen predators ...
Whaley-whale ... whaley-whale
All night he stares at the stars
winking on the sea-slopes
sea-slopes
mesmerising sea-slopes
bowing and bowing,
sea-slopes, sea-slopes,
mesmerising sea-slopes bowing
to the dim pink glow rising in the east.
Fade ...

To blackness dark down in the deep.
Whale-momma pale-grey
smiling in the smooth,
nonchalantly pleasant in her awesome power,
she strokes her flipper,
soft like a momma's arm,
ushering her calf-whale shy of the light,
rising up from blackness to dark green sea,

her flipper, like a momma's arm,
ushering, protecting, nursing her young,
and smiling,
smi - ling she smiled ...
ka-chinka-ching ...
ka-chinka-chinka ...
ka-chinka-chinka-chinka -

Whale! Roars George in the baby dawn.
- Whale! Whale! Strike the sails! Lower the
boats!
Pulla rigga-ropey rigga-ropey rigga-ropey
run the boats down:
One splash! Two splash!
Sleepy sailors slip on the deck
pulling on their boots
but Pawnee stops to look.
- No whale, he say, the captainman dream!
Second Mate Da Silva pauses on the gunwhale.
George pulls him down on the deck.

George: Take charge of the Catalpa Mister Da Silva. I'll
              take to the whaleboat.

He jumps.
The crewmen cheer.

George: It's a race! My boat against Mr. Smith's!

- Gauntlet accepted, roars Samuel Smith.

George: Sink the oars, bend your backs, pull, men, pull!
              Sink the oars, bend your backs, pull together
              men, pull!
              Sink the oars, bend your backs, pull together
              men - stop! *(Pause)*
              Raise your oars men! Raise your oars!

Smith's boat pulls ahead and the crewmen cheer
into the faraway waves ...
Pawnee say in a low tone
- What race they win when there no whale to
kill?

Pawnee shake the head. He sigh. He yawn.

Mopsy: Ssh! Mopsy see the captain's lips movin'. The others think he prayin', but Mopsy hear the magic, Mopsy hear the spell -

George stands at the prow of the boat, arms outstretched.

George: So you know ... wherefore you go ...
you'll never sail ... these seas again ...

(Music - whale surfacing)
Whale!
Mopsy throws the iron -
it buries itself in the flesh of her side
 a yard behind the eye,
under her flipper the whalecalf brushes the boat
but it stays upright as the harpoon rope unwinds
runna-rigga runna-rigga runna-rigga snake -
Pawnee falters, steps on the rope - fwip!
- Ah Paw - nee ...
hangs by his boot from a knot in the rope
'til the whale dives deep.
George seizes the axe.
He cuts the rope - patchunk!
- Too late.
Then, they hear a noise,
an angry noise of horses,
a million horses neighing, angry and wild!
(Music swell)
Mopsy bless himself.

Mopsy: It come from the whale, Captainman! A sperm whale! Poor Pawnee.

They search the sea with the oars,
but Pawnee gone down.
Pawnee who say there was no whale.
Poor Pawnee who yawn.
Smith's boat harpoons the calfwhale
and Brava makes the kill
- Good man Brava!

The boats draw together as the baby's blood
spreads.
They wait, they wait,
they wait until the mother-whale surfaces
shuddering and bawling,
George sinks the lance-
(Music sound effect)
to silence her still at last.
From her sea-flooding lungs her final sound -
(Music sound effect)
You prom - issed me ... you ... prom .. issed
me ...
Blood fills the sea.

Whaley-whale lash lash!
Whaley-whale lash lash!
Mother and daughter smiling still
belly-up are tied each side
in the grip of the happy Catalpa.
The flencing begins.
They rip the strips of blubber
off the naked meat beneath.
George laughs.
- I'm a whaleman, as much as anyone here!
Whaley-whale flence flence
whaley-whale flence flence
Nightime.
George stands in the glow of the boiler-fire
watching Mopsy and Toby
scoop the precious spermaceti
from the mother's skull
and stow it into kegs.
Their feet seem to speak
with the suction of the stuff.
- Prom - issed me ... prom - issed me ...
Mopsy looks at Toby.
But Mopsy and Tobey grin.
- The captainman - he can hear the whale-hum!
Whaley-whale whaley-whale
whaley -

Smith: Sorry to disturb you Captain Anthony. What I came to say is this. I saw today skill at the whalehunt such as I have never seen in my twenty years at sea. I'll follow you to Hell and back, Captain Anthony. That's what I came to say.

George: I'm glad you've reached that conclusion Mister Smith. Because that is precisely what I'm asking you to do.

Smith: Eh?

George: There'll be no more whaling 'til we've left Hell behind.

Smith: We've taken more than eighty barrels in less than a day Sir!

George: We'll deposit them in the Azores in two days time. We'll take far more than eighty barrels on our return - from Hell.

Smith: Where's Hell, Captain Anthony?

George: Fremantle. Western Australia.

Smith: We'd better take care how we broach the subject to the crew, Sir!

George: I'll leave that to you, Mister Smith.

(Music)
Ka-chinka-ching ka-chinka-ching
Cranston, Darragh, Hassett, Hogan, Harrington, and Wilson:
The freedom ship is on its way under Anthony's command ...
Didgeridoo de didgeridoo woo-woh-woo
Didgeridoo de didgeridoo woo-woh-woo
Freedom ship ... freedom fwip ...
freedom ship ... freedom fwip ... gwawk ...

Fade down to black.

Interval.

ACT TWO

Lights up slowly on Australia.

> Didgeridoo de-didgeridoo woo-woh-woo ...
> Whoh-woh-woh didgeridoo de-didgeridoo woo-
> woh-woo
>
> Fwip fwip fwip fwip
> seabird in the sunset
> fwip fwip shadow on the glip-glap sea
> gliding in fwipping for the burnt-brown toast-
> coast
> fwip fwip fwip
> a yellow whaler just ahead
> bearing out to sea
> bank up and -
> wheel around the mast-top
> zoom in the cabin porthole ...
> First Mate Smith filling in the log of the Catalpa:

Smith: Nightfall, Good Friday, year of Our Lord
eighteen hundred and seventy-six:
Dropped the Captain close to the shore near
Bunbury port ...

> log log logga logga down the logbook ...
> Pan down the leg of the desk
> down through the chink in the deckboards
> to the dark down deep in the hold.
> ka-chinka-ching ka-chinka-ching

Mopsy: Bad magic on Catalpa Pawnee!
Ocean we sail! We kill no whale!
Whaleman I! No whale - no man Mopsy!
Don' do riggin'! Don' do watch! Don' do nuthin!
Then Tobey Brava Lopez start the grumblin.
Captainman rage!
Put Mopsy in the whalechains!
But I hear no magic!

I hear no whale-hum!
The magic got took back away from he!
So yo' kno'! Whe'fo' yo' go!
Yo' neve' sail see seas again!
Kachinka-ching! Kachinka-

Fwip fwip fwip fwip flap and
bank up over the surf and the sand-dunes -
dust-cloud down on the ruggedy road
zoom
down
duggeda-duggeda duggeda-duggeda
stage coach stage coach
jiggede-jaggede jaunting a-jing-jing
George
looking out the window hears the -
Gwawk!
Fwip fwip ...
freedom trippe freedom trippe freedom
trippeda-clip-clip.
Fade into
wideshot
dark, nearing dawn,
Holy Saturday Holy Saturday
stagecoach approache coach approache
tracking into mid-shot
paa-an with the galloping coach
clippa-cloppa clippa
Free - mantle mantle closeup whoa!

Tinkle tinkle knock knock porter in pyjamas
opens up

George: Apologies so late Mister Collins is expecting -

Up the stairs, down the hall,
knockeda knock-knock,
pause,
chup bolt chain and key

Breslin: *(In deep south "James Collins" accent)* My
good friend! Come in!

Key chain bolt and chup
ear to the door 'til - footsteps fade

Breslin: A Hell of an hour to be waking me up!
Suspicion enough as it is! What held you up
damn it man, you're two months late, I thought
you were shipwrecked! Cranston Darragh
Hassett Hogan Harrington and Wilson are
champin' at the bit for the past - feels like a
feckin' lifetime I've been keeping up that
Yankee act for so buckin' long! A terrible time
trying to keep them under the thumb and not to
be seen consorting or talking - spies on every
corner man a Hellhole here!

George: No time to lose Mr Bres -

Breslin: Collins! James shaggin' Collins! I'm a big rich
Yankee mining man, remember? I'm running out
of mineshafts fast! Suspicion rising man! I've
made so many proposals for so many mines
there'll be so many bloody boreholes in
Australia there'll be no bush left. Governor's
thrilled. Thinks I'm Mr. Moneybags. Waitin' for
his cut!

George: How do we spring the six from the gaol -

Breslin: No need. Sit down. Governor wined and dined
me. Tinkle-ding - singing rim - best of crystal
and fine cheroots ... "Where will I get the labor
to work my mines, Mr. Governor, sir?" says I.
"Mr. Collins" says he, "the prisoners can be
made available for work deemed necessary for
the colony's economy. Rest assured your mining
enterprises would be so deemed."
But then he drops his voice - listen to this -
"I don't mind telling you in confidence, Mr.
Collins, intelligence reports indicate an escape
attempt is planned."
- Now where the buckin Hell did that come
from!? -
"so", says he, "I've had to confine them within
the prison walls. But in view of your dynamic

interest in our colony, I've set them to their tasks
again so you can see for yourself how
industrious they are".
And out the gate he takes me in his governor's
trap.
"Look to the left" he says.
And there on my left are Cranston and Hassett
digging the governor's garden. Cranston stands
still staring. Eyes as big as dinner plates. Then
he drops to his knees bawling "Thanks be to
God" 'til Hassett gives him a dig of a pick.
Lucky for me the governor's thick. The men are
out working around the town in order to impress
me enough to take them on in my mineshafts.

George:	Good. I brought maps and tide-charts to help us plot the escape -
Breslin:	It has to be the day after tomorrow.
George:	Monday!? Impossible! It's not enough time.
Breslin:	Easter Monday holiday! Half the garrison will be at the regatta upriver in Perth. Otherwise it's suicide.
George:	This way it's suicide. I need more time.
Breslin:	Soon as I got your telegraph I tipped off the six. They're ready an' rarin' to go! Monday it is! This is the plan-

Knock-knock.

Breslin: Ye-es?

- It's Marie.

Chup bolt chain key

Breslin: I'm busy Marie, I'm discussing a mineshaft. *A toute a l'heure* ...

Key chain bolt chup.

Breslin: Servant-girl.

George: French?

Breslin: Yeah. *Elle s'appelle* Marie Tondut. Taken a bit of a shine to me. A delicate state of affairs George. She's got herself in trouble.

George: What kind of trouble?

Breslin: Jesus Christ! She's twenty-three. I thought she was up to the dodge.

George: Dodge?

Breslin: Gettin' off a stop before the terminus, but oh no! She's gone and snared me George. Paternity! I don't see what gives you the right to be looking so morally righteous. You're the one who was two months late! What's a man supposed to do when he's left high and dry!? The devil finds work for idle - hands when it's laid out on a plate on a platterdish man French dinner for two well what the Hell would you do!?

George: I came to talk about the escape -

Breslin: She says I talk in my sleep. I don't know what she's heard. I asked her but she just laughed, fiddling with my moustache. Maybe she's just very, very fond of me. Or fond of Yankee Collins. I don't fool myself she'd be falling in love with plain John Breslin. Too feckin' earthy for her.

George: Now listen! I have to get back on board Catalpa to pick the crew for the rescue boat - I'll have a whaleboat ready and waiting at Rockingham beach eighteen miles to the North. You get the prisoners there on Monday at noon.

Breslin: She knows I'm up to something. If she twigs she'll turn against me. A woman scorned, George - she could sabotage the rescue.

George: You've jeopardised the entire expedition -

Breslin: She could put us both in the slammer for up to
twenty years. Do you want to see your missus
again?

Cut to balcony, rising sliver of Saturday sun
still some moonlight on the water of the Swan,
gentle river, easing along, to the sea,
the sea Gretta the sea,
George looks, at the twists, and the - turns,
sets off down the hall
and up the rickety backstairs:

George: I knock on her door.
(Music)
She opens it wide, smiling brilliantly.
Her face drops when she sees it's me.
I ask can I come in?
She stands back, lets me pass.
I tell her I was in Mister Collins' room when she
knocked. I'm the captain of a whaling ship I say,
and Mister Collins has asked me to arrange a
berth for her to Sydney which I'm delighted to
provide. He's heavily engaged in a mining deal
right now, but he's due to follow her in three
days' time.
Her eyes glisten. I want to hold her, say some
French, get her to call me *Geo-orges* ....
She looks - wistful is the word I think, though I
don't know quite what it means.
She asks why he does not come to tell her this
himself ...
I say he sent me to make sure I met with her
approval. He didn't want to book her on a ship
who's captain she might not trust.
- Do I trust you? she asks.
I say that only she can answer that. But I submit
that I consider dishonesty the most ignoble
crime.
She dwells on that a moment ...
She asks me do I know she's carrying a life
inside her body ...
I try to look at the ceiling,

43

but her body,
she seems to be asking me to look at her -
body ...
She's wearing a - it's hot in Fremantle -
she's wearing something long, and white, and
made out of - thin stuff ...
Christ! I've been eleven months at sea!
- Collins' progeny, she says - *progene* ...
She asks me to imagine
what it must be like
to carry inside you
the growing issue
of the loins of one you love.
I think of laughing it off
but no,
soft silvery light,
shining in the window on her shoulder ...
The ceiling again,
so interesting, brown.
- No time to waste, I say. I'll pick her up
personally in a sail-rigged whaleboat down at
the Fremantle jetty tomorrow at dawn.
She grabs my hand.
She takes it slowly and holds it against - her
stomach,
her flesh like fire through the thin soft stuff.
- Tell me now, she says, does James love me? Is
he true? *La verite!*?
I feel her fingernails sharp on my hand, this
hand, on her smooth stomach underneath the
white thing.
- Does her big crazy *homme de mystere* mean
what he says, she asks!? Did he speak to me in
his day-talk or in his secret sleep-talk like a gruff
big gentle brown bear, she asks?
I hesitate,
my hand still there,
she, eyes glistening, fixed on mine,
I daren't look away, I want to lean in and kiss
her say forget the stupid fool I'll take you to
Sydney Marie look at me we'll go to sea now

we'll sail straight away we'll live in bliss I want
to say ... she's so - beautiful!
I hate him for it
Breslin I hate you you hear!?
But I mustn't falter now, man of duty, gave my
word, Gretta's patches a thing of the past, so you
know, ka-chinka-ching, wherefore you go, clear
where my duty lie, but I can feel a pain deep in
here as my mouth says what my heart withers to
hear.
- He talks about you, I say, as if he's in a dream.
My hand still there, I can feel the softness of her
spirit singing through her skin.
- He shed man's tears as he told me about the
first time he saw you, how it changed his life he
said -
She pulls her hand back, taken aback I can tell,
she seems shocked, what have I said!?
- He told you about ... under the kitchen table?
she asks, eyebrows high, and a little bit pleased
it seems to me, yes she's smiling, beautifully ...
- yes, the kitchen table, yes, he told me, I say,
smiling, as if it's - wistful, whatever wistful
means! Wistful! Wishing it was me, under the
kitchen table, anywhere at all with this truly the
most beautiful creature I have ever seen.
But I've taken my hand away, taken it back
again, I've done my duty, I've lied.
On the back of her door hangs a long muslin
shawl.
It brushes my hand.
She smiles.
Sourire ...
- You have honest eyes, *Georges*. I'll trust you
on the sea ...

Fwip fwip fwip time passing tic tic
Cut to George back on board Catalpa
Easter Sunday evening dark down in the hold:

George: Mopsy! I've taken off your chains. I know you
think I'm cruel. But I'm not! Everything I've

done on this voyage I've done in the cause of
freedom from cruelty.
I'm launching the whaleboat to go ashore. Some
- stuff to fetch. We'll need to be fast. I need **you**
to steer us.

Mopsy: Whaleman Mopsy! No whale, no man Mopsy!

George: One short voyage in the whaleboat Mopsy! Just
one! Then we'll kill so many whales you'll
collect the biggest purse you've ever seen. And
so will I. I guarantee it Mopsy. I give you my
word.

Shadow behind. Silhouette on deckboards. Hitch
- cock - ! Somebody listening.

Mopsy: What - stuff we goin' into land to fetch, Mister
Captain sir?

George: Some crewmen Mopsy. Extra crew. That's all.

Mopsy: Then we whalemen again?

George: Then you and I will be whalemen again. I
brought you some breadfruit and a pound of
ham. Eat!

Up the laddera brung - brung - brung -
Sudden scuffle
Closeup hand on George's mouth.
Dragged into the dark.

George: Duggan! What the Hell are -

Duggan: I'm comin' in the whaleboat.

George: Return to your post! I command this mission as
long as we're at sea.

Duggan: Not when you're dealing with a member of the
IRB!

George: This was all agreed! Devoy gave me his
commitment -

Duggan: Devoy's my commander! I take my orders from
him! Direct! I'm comin' ashore!

George: Can't you count!? Thirteen in a whaleboat made
for six! One more is madness! You'll kill us all!

Cut to the deck: Whaleboat droppeda ropeda
splash-wash.
Tobey Brava Lombard and Kanaka man the oars.
Mopsy mans the steer.
Duggan scrambles down, sits in the middle, feet
around the food and water.
George turns to First Mate Smith.

George: If we don't return by first light Tuesday, sail the
Catalpa back to New Bedford, Mr. Smith. Take
this letter to my wife, Gretta.

Smith: I'll do your bidding sir. Though I pray I shall
never have to.

George shakes last hands with First Mate Smith.
Men about to part in peril makes them want
to - hug.
But they don't. Down jumps George.

George: Sink the oars, bend your backs, pull, men -

Cut: Interior: Hotel:
Folded sheet of paper slips under Breslin's door.

Breslin: Perfume of jasmine.
Imprint of lips.
Wait until I'm sure she's gone before I pick it up.
Stand still and listen.
Her little bare footsteps away down the hall...
Unfold.
I want to tell you,
once in my life I want to tell you so you'll
always know,
my heart bursts with joy, my big brown Yankee
bear,
to be the bearer of the bringer of your future joy.
You'll be an old gran-papa,

I can see you, still a big old patched-up bear,
with your sealion moustache which seems to
talk all by itself,
a young girl will ask you
to tell her yet again
the story of the time you travelled to West
Australia
and met her grand-mama in the middle of the
night
when she was a serving-girl
sitting at the kitchen-table of an old hotel.
You'll smile, sitting in your armchair,
somewhere in Sydney town,
across from you I'll still smile that smile
that you say reminds you of the babbling creeks
of Wicklow - Arkansaw.
I'll smile for you in Sydney, James,
I'll meet you on the pier,
I'll tell you how I love you
with your big bear arms all around me, James,
I'll be waiting,
your everlasting love,
Je t'embrace,
Marie Tondut.
(Pause)
To the lamp, Marie Tondut, nothing I can do but
consign you to the whale-oil lamp, and all I can
say is that this heart, John Breslin's heart, is as
close to breaking as it's possible for John
Breslin's heart to be.

Cut to a wideshot of the sea-shore, dark:
whaleboat glip-glapping to the empty beach,
cut to the prow shallow-wallow shingle-shingle
shunt!

George: Good work men. Get some sleep. It's nearly -

Cut:
Dawn.
In the hotel stables

Breslin hitches a resident's trap to the owner's
team of four.
Tschish!
Clippeda-cloppeda clippeda-cloppeda
down the lane and out the gate
and clip into Fremantle town
clippeda-cloppeda clippeda-cloppeda
Thanks be to God it's a holiday jolliday
Not very many about -
except for the prisoners starting their work
shovels and picks shovels and picks
Cranston and Hassett are digging their rill
chiggeda-chuh chiggeda-chuh
clippeda-cloppeda clippeda-cloppeda
hup! Lie under the sacks!
Clippeda-cloppeda clippeda-cloppeda
so far so good
nobody caring to look -
clippeda-cloppeda clippeda-cloppeda
Hogan and Darragh are building a shed
at the back of the sexton's yard
clippeda-cloppeda clippeda-cloppeda
running-jump over the wall and they dive!
Into the trap and on top of the sacks!
Fucketa pucketa boot in me back!
Clippeda-cloppeda clippeda-cloppeda

Breslin: People looking sideways!
             Cut the bucking crap!

Clippeda-cloppeda clippeda-cloppeda
Wilson and Harrington cutting the bush
back at the southern end of the town
clippeda-clopppeda clippeda-cloppeda
walk away clippeda-cloppeda
over the field clippeda-cloppeda
Hup! Tschish!
Duggeda-duggeda duggeda-duggeda
kick up a bucketa muckedan puckedan
rocket along on their way,
to Rockingham Bay ...
to Rockingham Bay...

Tschish!

Cut:
To Rockingham Beach:
chuff chuff chuff
closeup George alone,
picks up a stone ...

George: The sound of the sea ... the sound of the sea ...
down at the Fremantle jetty,
a woman with a suitcase,
wearing a muslin shawl,
stands still,
staring,
eyes out to sea,
waiting,
for the captain with the honest eyes
to come in his whaleboat
and take here away -
with the sound of the sea ...
to Sydney Marie ...
to Sydney with me ...

Cut:
To the Rockingham road:
A-duggeda duggeda duggeda duggeda
Nation Once Aduggeda duggeda duggeda
duggeda
Nation Once Aduggeda duggeda
Cut:
To Rockingham Beach:

George: He's just a vacant fool.

Duggan: No he's not. What's he watchin' us for?

George: Leave this to me Duggan! That's an order!

Duggan: We're not on the Catalpa now Anthony! I'm
Fenian commander until Breslin comes! And I
say that man has seen us, he's suspicious, and he
must be done away with!

George: Stay with the crew!

Duggan: I'm comin' with yeh!

            Chuff chuff chuff chuff

George: Good morning.

Man   Mornin'!

George: What brings you here?

Man: Nothing in particular. How 'bout you?

George: Just waiting.

Man: Waiting for what!?

George: Midday.

Man: Yeah!? What happens at midday?

George: The eh- the noonbell strikes.

Man: What you planning to put in the whaleboat!?

            Duggan strolls nonchalantly behind the
            inquisitive fool. The gleam of a dagger in hand -

Man: You're smuggling something! Tell the truth!

            Duggan raises the dagger to -

George: (To Duggan) Stop! I order you to drop it!

Man: (Replying) Okay. Consider it dropped.

            Sudden the thumping of faraway hooves:-
            Duggeda duggeda duggeda - whoa!

Duggan: Breslin! We've been seen! We've got to finish
            him!

George: Very well Mister Duggan. Take command of the
            whaleboat! Navigate it back to the Catalpa!

Duggan: He'll inform on us! We've got to slit his throat!

George: The man will not be harmed! Else the whaleboat
            will not sail!

Duggan: What are you goin' to do about it Breslin!?

Breslin: Duggan! give the fool a shillin' and send him to
the pub! George! launch the whaleboat!

George: Very well. All hands to the gunwhales! Heave!

Shingle shingle shallow wallow schluck-luck

George: Rescued prisoners lie in the boat! Duggan and
Breslin get down there too. Stay out of the way
of the crew!

Launch ... surge ... plunge ... surge ... plunge ...
surge ...

Duggan: Look! Back on the beach! Old Curiosity's
turnin' the trap and whippin' the horses back
towards town! I told yeh Breslin! We should
have slit the bastard's throat! He'll squeal!
They'll set a bloody battleship on us! We
haven't a chance!

George: Wrong Duggan! We'll be on the Catalpa before
he reaches town. She'll outstrip any steamship.
All we need is a little bit of wind.

Fwip ... fwip ... fwip ... fwip

Cut to Catalpa ten miles out:
Smith looks up at the sails.
Not a flap. Not a billow. Not a creak.

Smith: This is not natural. The calm before the -

Crow's nest:
- Storm comeeng Meester Smeeth!
Bree - ee - eeze flappeta-flap-flap ...

Smith: Mr. Da Silva! Mainsail! Topsail! Spanker and
jib! Out to sea before she breaks or we'll be
driven in onto the cliffs!

Cut to the whaleboat pulling out from the shore:
Plunge - surge ... plunge -

Bree - ee - eeze splasheta splosh-losh!

George: I can see the Catalpa's topsail.

But: there's something else big looming up
behind!
Now we see what Smith in the Catalpa saw:
The Big Wide Special Effect Shot:
Storm Blowing In From Antartica!
- Holy Mother of -
Pan across as thirteen pairs of eyes turn to look
at -
Closeup George.

George: Take cheer men! You're almost free! We'll get to
the Catalpa before the storm breaks!

The dark shadow of stormclouds covers his face
like a veil.
Tobey Brava Lombard and Kanaka
Oars sink! Oars sink!
The prisoners bucket and bail!

But it's Too Late!
Storm: Breaks!
(Music)
The tiny whaleboat jumps and jars!
The Symphony of Storm!
Bern - stein! Bern - stein!
Phosphorescence flickers!
Aurora! Aurora Australis!
Pictures in the storm-clouds!
A giant apparition:
Gretta's mother on her deathbed:

Momma-in-
the-Wind: You promised me ....
you'd never go to sea,
she loves you dangerously, dangerous you see?

Flickering snakes! A muslin shawl,
stretching to infinity from Fremantle jetty:

Apparition Two:

Marie-in-the-Storm:	You have honest eyes Georges I'll trust you on the sea ... *Donnez-moi la main qui a touche* Marie Tondut!
George:	I meant you no harm! I did it for freedom Marie! Ah! Hand flenced by the raging rope, the hand that touched her stomach is ripped red ragged and raw. More! More storm! Flashes of crimson silk: A blinding apparition: Gretta on the landing in the skies:
Gretta-in-the-Skies:	You've chosen the sea. Unfaithful man! You'll never sail these seas again! *Adieu!*
George:	*(shouts)* Gretta forgive me! She smiled ... underneath the bonnet lace ... Storm whips the chinka-ching chains from George's bleeding hand - splash underwater the chains go down slo - mo to the soft sea bed. Cut to the blazing sun. The half-sunken whaleboat rocking in the sea, full of slumped still bodies ... George still gripping the steer. Zoom in to a slowly rising head:
Breslin:	George ... ?
George:	We're done for, Mr. Breslin. Just the battleship coming for us now. Twenty years I think you said.

Breslin:	Twenty years my backside! The Catalpa's comin' to save us!
George:	No! I've been a fool. I should have swum ashore back in New Bedford - back to Gretta on the quayside - nuts, bolts, screws -
Breslin:	George!
George:	I ordered Smith to sail her home first light today.
Breslin:	Slap the gurrier in irons! He disobeyed a command. Because here comes Catalpa!

Fourteen pairs of eyes peer over the prow.
- Hauh ... !
But is it that easy!? Oh no!

Mopsy: Mopsy see smoke Captainman!

Smoke astern.The battleship Georgette.
Steaming for Catalpa.
The whaleboat directly in between.
Cut to the chase!
The formula shots.
Georgette enormous in the frame
shugga-shugga shugga-shugga
whale-boat whale-boat
Catalpa Catalpa Ca-flappeta-flappeta ...
Georgette shugga-shugga foghorn foghorn!
Whale-boat whale -

Slam-Catalpa-cachunk!

George: Climb the sideboards men!
Hoist the stars and stripes Mr. Smith!

Smith: Ay ay Captain! Hoist the ensign!
Pulla-rigga-ropey rigga-ropey flagga-wagga
high!
She's turning her guns on us sir!

George: Not possible! The stars and stripes protect us!

Bwaaw!

Cannonball across the bows!

Georgette: *(To tune of God Save The Queen)*
Captain heave to or we'll
blow the masts out of you,
heave to, heave to!

George on the poopdeck, speaking-trumpet
poised:

George: *(To tune of Star Spangled Banner)*
The American flag,
I am on the high seas.
Fire on this ship,
and you fire on the American flag!

George: Let's get the wind behind us!

Wheel into the westward tack, the sails billow
and fill,
Catalpa's away! Catalpa's away!

George: Ireland Boys: Hurray!

(To tune of Deep In Canadian Woods)
Catalpa's on her way
Slán Australia! Slán Australia!
Ireland Boys - hurray!

Pull back and rise for
sundry sea-shots,
Catalpa riding the waves.
Fade into celebration banquet at sea:
Canned chicken and tinned fruit,
and a feed of boiled potatoes for
Cranston Darragh Hassett Hogan Harrington and
Wilson.

The Six: Ireland boys hurray! Ireland boys hurray!
We'll cheer for Anthony! Dear old Anthony!
Anthony boys - hurray!

Mopsy: Now Mopsy goin' to kill the whale Pawnee!

> Now Mopsy goin' to kill the whale!
> The captainman goin' to do his ching kachinka
> ching
> And Mopsy goin' to kill the whale!

The Six: Ireland boys hurray! Ireland boys hurray!

The Crew: Whaley-whale ... whaley-whale
whaley -

Cut to the deck: Night: Duggan at large.

Duggan: Cranston! Darragh! Hassett! Hogan! Harrington! Wilson!
There's a Fenian convention in New York City in two months time. I know you six will want to be there to support Mr. Devoy. No time for whalin' lads! The Catalpa sails straight for New York!

Whaley-whale ... whaley-whale ...

Breslin: Have you changed course, George? The rescued men are agitated. They say you've changed course for the North Atlantic whaling grounds.

George: As agreed Mr. Breslin.

Breslin: I'm with you all the way George, but the men - understandable after ten years in chains - I'm sorry George, but I have to tell you they want to be brought straight to New York. All six are unanimous George. And Duggan of course. Let me be honest - I have a revolt on my hands. I can't isolate myself and let a hothead the like of Duggan take command. I can't risk a split! Slap bang in our moment of triumph! I have no option George. I **have** to take the men straight to New York!

George: I don't see how Mr. Breslin. I'm captain of the Catalpa and I say the Catalpa is going to whale.

Breslin: Don't force me to do what I dread!

57

George:	Two weeks' whaling Mr. Breslin! No debate! I require five hundred barrels to fulfil my commitments.
Breslin:	What commitments?
George:	I'm paid by captain's percentage. I'm not going home empty-handed. I can't. Neither will my crew.
Breslin:	Your commitment then is to money. My commitment is to a far higher cause.
George:	Commitment is a quality I think you know little about!
Breslin:	Nobody questions my commitment! Not you! Nobody!
George:	Where's your commitment to Marie Tondut, Mister Big Brown Hairy Bear Collins!? Don't you think you ought to change course for Sydney, Mister Kitchen Table Mining Speculator!?
Breslin:	She told you about - under the kitchen table? What could I do George? A man can't live forever in an artificial skin. Collins will always love her. But I have a commitment to the cause of - freedom. Please, George, I'm begging you, please change course voluntarily for New York Harbour!
George:	I'm whaling before we cast anchor, Mr. Breslin. I'm whaling for the last time, and nobody is going to stop me. Not you! Nobody!
Breslin:	Damn you! The men are waitin'! Duggan's lookin' for his chance! He'll topple me! He'll arrest you! He'll confine you to your quarters! And then both of us, after all we've sacrificed, after all we've achieved, will both be broken men!

(Music)
Nightime. Starlight.

Bwaawp! Bwaawp!
Pilot tugs Catalpa tugga-tugga
past Coney Island tugga-tugga
up The Narrows
round Robbins' Reef tugga-tugga
past ... Liberty Island, Ellis Island,
and into Upper Bay
Fwip fwip fwip fwip
seabird
settles on the mainmast
Bwaawp!
Catalpa casts her anchor - splash!
New York Harbour, 2am, August 19th, 1876.

Breslin: You did the right thing George.

George: As any prisoner would, Mister Breslin.

Gwaawk!
Seabird flaps its wings and takes flight
up into the yardy air
over the twinkling wavelets - tschish -
to the lanterns lining the docks
and up over and in between
the dim speckled tenements of Manhattan West
circling above the glow of the gaslamps ...
Dissolve magically to daylight: The Bowery.
The Bowery The Bowery
The Bowery The Bowery
crowds cheering line the streets - yahoo! -
clerks in the dingy offices far above
scatter their scratch-paper down
like - snowflakes falling
New York has never seen its like
somebody coins a name -
the ticker-tape parade
the ticker-tape parade
as the Bowery bands of Hibernia
batter the hides of the Big Base -
Zoom down onto a balcony,
The O'Donovan Rossa Hotel:

CATALPA

Devoy: Devoy devoy devoy devoy de - ladies and
          gentlemen, the moment you have all been
          waiting for! The six gallant sons of Erin are
          about to stand before you! But first, the unsung
          hero of the valiant rescue, free men everywhere
          are forever in his debt, put your hands together a
          cháirde, bualadh bos, fáilte mór, beir bua go
          brách for that great champion of justice and
          freedom - Mister - John Breslin!

Breslin: Thank you John. Well, there is one man whom
          I'd like to thank for our celebrations here today.
          That man is Captain George Anthony, of New
          Bedford Massachussetts, a man of the utmost
          integrity and commin - ... contiment- ...
          contimentment?

Devoy: Come on Breslin! Come on! Devoy devoy
          devoy devoy de- here they are now, the
          Fremantle Six, an-seo inár muidne, tá bród orm
          an seisear iontach seo a chur in aithne daoibh -
          Cranston Darragh Hassett Hogan Harrington
          agus -

          Gwawk!
          Fwip fwip fwip fwip
          rise to the west
          fwip fwip
          Over the streets
          clogged with the crazy crowds
          bird's eye view of
          Mopsy on a corner

Mopsy: Roll up! Roll up!

          People jostle for view:

Mopsy: One dollar for a relic of the rescue ship Catalpa.
          Roll up! Pieces cut from the yellow gunwhale!
          Mwuh! Mopsy kill the dollar whale!

          Steam-engine George phoo puffa-puffa
          chuffa-chuffa tracka-tracka
          chuffa-chuffa tracka-tracka

Gretta-Gretta I'm back-I'm backa
Gretta-Gretta I'm back-I'm backa

Passenger: Wow! What a sensation! What a daring rescue! I say! Have you heard about this whaling ship!?

George: No. I know nothing about it.

Crier: Fall River! Fall River!

Door tinkle-ding.

Shop Lady: Can I help you sir?

George: A bar of lemon soap please.

Shop Lady: Wrapped for the lady-love?

George: No! Just - give me the soap please!

Knock-knock.

George: Pardon me ma'am. I was wondering if I could pay you for the use of your tub, and some hot water.

Ribs. An old man's ribs.
Hair. Dry grey wisp.
Eyes. Bloodied and bagged.
Try to rub - the smell - of whaleship - off my body. It's deep in the bones.
The palm of my hand - rope-scarred.
The smell of the sea - coming through the lemon soap. The smell of the -

Boy: New Bedford stagecoach! Stagecoach for New Bedford!

Clippeda-cloppeda down the hill
past the Richardsons' mansion,
lawns perfectly smooth,
clippeda-cloppeda down and round the
corkscrew bend
to the waterfront,

the quayside,
fwip fwip fwip fwip,
clippa-slip one of the horses slips on the
cobblestones,
she smiled,
underneath the bonnet lace,
Clippa-cloppa whoa!
Round the pawnshop corner.
Door needs paint.
Wood is warping.
Should I knock?
No, it's on the latch. Just push ...
Grandfather clock, not ticking, stopped.
Forgot to wind. Or maybe mislaid the key.
Stairs.
Halfway up.
Brown eyes. A crimson dress, patched at the
hem.
Two pigtails. The length of her hair!
She's holding a doll.
She's calling her - Marie ...
She twirls the smiling doll making her dance.

George: Hello, Pearl.

Stands, turns, up the stairs carefully,
maybe told not to run,
says slowly and softly through the banister bars

Pearl: Momma, I think it might be Poppa.

Lighting changes to
Matthew Kidd's bedsit.

Slow fade to black.

THE END.